When We Don't See It

When We Don't See It

Poems by

Jennifer Lagier

© 2025 Jennifer Lagier. All rights reserved.
This material may not be reproduced in any form, published,
reprinted, recorded, performed, broadcast,
rewritten or redistributed without
the explicit permission of Jennifer Lagier.
All such actions are strictly prohibited by law.

Cover design by Shay Culligan
Cover image by Guzman Barquin on Unsplash
Author photo by Oliver Fellguth

ISBN: 978-1-63980-824-3

Kelsay Books
502 South 1040 East, A-119
American Fork, Utah 84003
Kelsaybooks.com

for Kate & Laura

Acknowledgments

Thank you to the following publications, where versions of these poems previously appeared.

Beach Chair Press: "Swimming Out of My Dreams"
Dear O Deer: "Recovery"
The Five-Two: "Hate Crime," "Shadow Government."
Formidable Woman Sanctuary: Journal of Literature & Art by "Sacred Space"
Medusa's Kitchen: "Fiscalini Ranch Birding," "Hummingbirds at Sunrise," "Sunset Dinner at Happy Talk Bar & Grill," "Willing Suspension of Disbelief," "Tunnel of Moonlight," "February Transition"
Monterey Poetry Review: "Smudge,"
New Verse Review: "Fluidity"
Raven's Perch: "Remembering How to Fly" & "Windmills"
The Rockford Review: "Conundrum," "Bremerton-1970," "Winter Solstice"
Song of the San Joaquin: "Scarlet Reminders," "Crows," "Sodden Spring"

Thank you to Diane Frank, Kate Aver Avraham, and Laura Bayless for their editorial assistance.

Contents

FLASHBACK

Pasta Prodigy	15
On the Beach	16
Low Rent	17
What Is Broken	19
I Am One of Them	21
Relocation	22
Bremerton—1970	24
Washburn's General Store	25
S.S. Titanic	27
Grandma	29
Born to Be Wild	30
Visitation	32
Blood and Memories	34
Euthanasia	35
Flashback	36
Meditation	38
Clearing Out	39
The Boxed-Up Dream	40
Diatribes from the Afterlife	41
Swimming Out of My Dreams	42

THE REAL STORY

Communion of Clumsy Sisters, Stumbling Souls	47
Antidote	48
Gaza 2023	49
Hate Crime	50
Winter Solstice	51
Illumination	52

Imagine	53
Peace Lanterns	54
Shadow Government	55
Smudge	56
Storm Front	57
The Real Story	59
A Cold Coyote Always Returns	60
Where Trickster Lurks	62
Tarnished Grail	63
Fractured Fairytale	64
Windmills	65

WHEN WE DON'T SEE IT

When We Don't See It	69
Shivering and Shedding	70
Washing Death Out of Your Ears	71
Consider Yourself Lucky	72
Road Trip	73
Fluidity	74
Heat Dome	75
Rockaway Ramble	76
Shivers	78
The Graduate	79
Entering the Temple of Words	80
Her Barefooted Gypsy Soul	81
The Only Train in Town	82
February Transition	84
Remembering How to Fly	85
Conundrum	86
Summons	87

Sunset Dinner at Happy Talk Bar & Grill	88
Ichabod Egret	89
Incel	90
Rainy Day Rooster	91
What Is Unseen	92

SACRED SPACE

Autumn Avalanche	95
Super Moon	96
Pre-Dawn Meditation	97
Sodden Spring	98
Morning's Surprise	99
Embezzlement	100
Wetland Concert	101
Garden of Weedin'	102
Scarlet Reminders	103
Liberation	104
Sacred Space	105
Hummingbirds at Sunrise	106
Crows	107
Fiscalini Ranch Birding	108
Sun Dog	109
First Light	110
Tunnel of Moonlight	111
Recovery	112
Willing Suspension of Disbelief	113

FLASHBACK

*You pay for what you get, you own what you pay for . . .
and sooner or later whatever you own
comes back home to you.*
—Stephen King, *It*

Pasta Prodigy

My Italian grandmother
taught me how to make pasta.
She'd pour a mountain of flour
onto wood kitchen table,
add a pinch of salt, dollop of olive oil,
mix in an egg and knead
until silky dough turned bright yellow.

We'd take turns using the rolling pin
to stretch, flatten the stiff lump
into a thin sheet dusted with semolina
which she'd coil, slice into satiny ribbons.
Uncurled noodles dried on a clean dish towel
until boiled, topped with garlicky tomato sauce,
grated Asiago cheese, a sprinkle of parsley.

All afternoon, we'd lovingly prepare
and assemble our delectable dinner,
serve it with crusty French bread,
salad with radishes, lettuce,
and tomatoes straight from the garden.

Today I feel her presence standing beside me,
hear broken English instructions
as I work at my stone counter.
Strong hands reach from the past
pilot my fingers.

On the Beach

Every summer we caravanned
from Central Valley orchards
to Santa Cruz beachfront,
cars filled with folding chairs, towels,
aunts, uncles, cousins.

My grandmother brought iced tea,
jugs of sugary red Kool Aid
enhanced with pungent pineapple juice.
Mom packed an ice chest
with potato salad, watermelon,
greasy fried chicken.

We staked out territory
at boardwalk's edge
near carnival rides
and late afternoon shade
it would provide
for the painfully sunburnt.

All day we collected broken shells,
waded into salty surf,
let muscular breakers pummel us.
Spiraling seaweed fragments levitated
as rising winds formed tornados of sand.

Low Rent

I grew up in a house
built as budget permitted,
one room at a time,
chicken wire poking
through crude plaster,
walls out of plumb.

We lived just outside
a jerkwater town,
near a noisy cannery,
peach grading station,
open irrigation canal.

During windstorms,
drifting Delta peat dust
smudged the horizon,
carried spores of Valley Fever
into our lungs.

Frost glazed bare limbs,
froze mud puddles.
Tule fog erased
orchards, moving cars,
the highway's dotted
white center line.

High school boys I dated
lifted our broken doors
back onto rusty hinges,

tried to repair our untended home,
replaced rotten fenceposts.

They mistakenly assumed
I would pay off
like a winning slot machine
in a jackpot of teenage gratitude sex.

What Is Broken

My aunt called with news
of my niece's death
in an accident less than a mile
from her grandparents' home
where she was spending the summer.
Three hours away, making dinner,
I insisted it must be a mistake.

My father blamed himself
because he bought the car
that ended her life,
skull impaled on rear view mirror
as her vehicle,
t-boned by a speeding teenager,
rolled down an embankment.

At the wrecking yard,
I was the one who salvaged
gore-spattered toolbox, electric typewriter,
stained gym clothes and shoes,
scrubbed what I could,
tossed all the rest.

Running errands, I broke down
at the grocery checkout counter
when I saw her signature
from the previous day
on my parent's charge account ledger.

The store owner took me outside,
put his around me,

wept as he described
his daughter's recent suicide.

You never completely heal, he told me,
you just learn to endure,
survive holidays
with that empty chair
at your table.

I Am One of Them

It was 1969,
a summer of date-rape
mislabeled free love.

The guy was
a friend of a friend.
I only knew him as John.
He invited me over
for a toke after work,
poured a glass of Red Mountain.

Even now, I feel him
blocking my screams,
using his mouth
as a weapon.

Stoned, I couldn't
fight back,
endured pain, humiliation,
seethed at becoming
one more of his victims.

After, I drove myself home,
smeared thick makeup
over visible bite marks,
scratches and bruises.

Never told a soul.
Still flinch from nightmares
of unwanted touching.

Relocation

After receiving orders for semi-isolated duty,
we pack pots, pans, and clothes,
shop for a mobile home
on the seedy side of Seattle.

We sell my sexy '67 Mustang,
buy a battered Ford station wagon,
invest in a two-bedroom trailer house
to be towed, ferried, then parked on a concrete slab
overlooking Straits of Juan de Fuca
and Vancouver Island.

During the trip to Cape Flattery,
a huge pothole near Forks
collapses a wheel on our new trailer.
Crews come, fix the damage.
For hours, we drive through Olympic Forest,
along dirt and gravel roads,
finally cross a cattle guard,
enter the Makah Reservation
just before dusk.

That first night we sleep
in a borrowed camper.
Just after daybreak, men settle
our home on concrete blocks,
install plywood siding,
hook us up to water and propane.

There is no telephone,
sketchy electrical power.

For three lonely years,
the Clallam County Bookmobile,
tea and pinochle with other Coast Guard wives,
working part-time at Elvrum's Café
and Washburn's General Merchandise Store
keep me from going insane.

Bremerton—1970

We drive three hours
along a winding, one lane road
through dense Olympic rain forest
from the Makah Reservation
to the Bremerton base.

We traverse football-length Quonset huts
crammed with amputees,
limbless soldiers shipped stateside
from the Viet Nam war.
Bandaged, maimed men
crowd rows of hospital beds
in multiple wards.

Those who still possess an arm,
a few fingers, reach out to touch
as I shudder and pass.
The ones with head injuries
are wrapped in white gauze shrouds,
lay silent and motionless.

My routine bloodwork and medical consultation
now seems a waste of resources.
Around us, wounded battalions
face a multitude of obstacles,
may never recover,
will endure years of PTSD.

Washburn's General Store

Makah Reservation, 1969–1972

At the town's only store,
we accepted American and Canadian money,
food stamps, scavenged glass fishing floats,
freshly caught salmon, cedar baskets,
Native American beadwork and carvings.

As a cashier,
I worked one of two registers,
knew customers by name
and family lineage.

When the girl who pulled a baby
through snow in a lug box arrived,
I would cuddle her infant,
sometimes slip her a dollar or two
to cover the cost of groceries.

Over time, I learned to cut glass,
sell stove pipe, fishing gear,
restock shelves,
order rope and hardware,
dust every counter.

Once during closing,
I locked the door,
bagged cash and coins from the tills,
slammed it and a finger
under heavy iron door of the floor safe.

Time throbbed.
My smashed digit blackened and bled
as I drifted in and out of consciousness,
worked the combination lock
to extricate trapped appendage.
I broke a bone, lost a nail,
worked the rest of the week
with swollen hand in a bandage.

S.S. Titanic

We follow a crude map
drawn onto a cocktail napkin,
abandon our car by a fallen tree,
hike sodden trail through Olympic Forest
saturated by 140 inches of annual rainfall.
At path's end, we discover
an ancient rowboat tied to rickety pier,
spring-fed pond fringed by acres
of towering cedars.

My husband paddles the tiny skiff
across stagnant reservoir.
Water sluices through leaky floorboards,
pools around soggy ankles.
Splashing oars displace algae,
submerged frogs, floating lilies.
Pan sized trout kiss the intersection
of gnat-filled air and wind-propelled ripples.

We sit for hours, curse our inability
to catch even one fish
despite seething schools
that bump worm-laden hooks
but never swallow the bait.

Trudging back to our station wagon,
we frighten a mother grizzly and her cubs
who crash past us through undergrowth.
I remember reading how bears

will flee when encountering fire.
On high alert, I brandish silver lighter
and greasy lunch bag for protection,
ready to torch crumpled paper.

Grandma

She was our commanding officer's mom,
stood six feet, two inches tall,
wore men's size twelve oxfords.
Formerly a cook at an Alaskan lumber camp,
she ran the kitchen at Elvrum's Café,
intimidated her quiet Makah assistant,
taught me verbal shorthand
to call out my orders,
carry two full plates on each arm
to customers at Formica tables.

I served as a waitress in training,
worked the milkshake machine,
swept floors, brewed coffee,
bantered with airmen from the SAC base,
answered tourists' questions,
washed pots, dishes, and glasses.

At night, she helped me
fend off drunken fishermen,
haul black plastic garbage sacks
out to the trash bin.

As a sweet reward, she sent me home
with generous slices of blackberry pie,
cups of soft vanilla ice cream,
my share of tips from the pickle jar
displayed on the counter.

Born to Be Wild

Just back from Vietnam, not willing
to endure another separation,
my husband requested transfer
to a remote Coast Guard station
in Neah Bay at the tip of Cape Flattery.
Here he joined an assortment
of court-referred misfits.
We were assigned a trailer pad
with water and electrical hookups.

Unpaved roads,
140 inches of annual rainfall
left our red MG Midget immobile.
We replaced it with a second-hand
Harley Davidson chopper.

Its ape hanger handlebars,
orange fuel tank
emblazoned with an eyeball
and the letters L S D
made us look
like leather-jacketed badasses
as we varoomed around
the Makah Reservation.

Skidding along a muddy trail
deep in the Olympic Forest,
he lost balance, spilled us both,

ploughing my head
into the side of a mountain.
Despite a headache and scraped face,
I gave thanks for protective helmet.

Flying down the empty expanse
of Shi Shi Beach,
he braked suddenly
to avoid a silvery snarl of driftwood.
Jolted loose, I sailed over him and the bike,
skidded across packed sand on my elbows.

Back at our trailer house,
I showered, bandaged raw skin
as he drove our homicidal motorcycle
to meet its new owner.

Visitation

My parents drove from California ranch
to Cape Flattery on two lane highway
through thick cedar forest.
Just before entering the Makah Reservation,
they passed a wrecked pickup,
tribal police, several bloodied men.

Shaken, they arrived at our trailer house
perched beside a helicopter landing pad
overlooking breakwater-protected bay.
Across the Straits of Juan de Fuca,
the blue shadow of Vancouver Island.

Mom wanted to take us for dinner.
I explained the town had one tiny cafe,
now closed for the evening.
Instead, I cooked pasta with french bread,
served a limp commissary lettuce salad.
While we nibbled gingersnaps for dessert,
she nervously peered out the window.

Dispirited herds of feral horses and stray dogs
wandered dirt streets bordered
by ragged fishing shacks.
The rising moon silhouetted rats
as they leapt from car to car,
unending rows of rusted out junkers.

No restaurants. No shopping malls.
My mother wept at the bleakness.

That night a Medivac chopper woke us
at midnight to transport a pregnant neighbor
who needed a C-section to the Coast Guard Hospital
far away in Port Angeles.
My parents couldn't wait to leave,
head home to their familiar world
of orchards, coffee shops, conservative farmers.

Blood and Memories

Fifty years after a surprise Tet Offensive
he remembers hiding, unarmed,
beneath sacked supplies
at the edge of a Quonset hut.
When Viet Cong overran his base camp,
they catch him off-guard, weaponless.

Decades later, back in the world,
he sleeps fitfully beside me,
keeps a baseball bat under the bed,
dreams of blood, bullets, terror.
One fist clenches a razor-sharp K-bar knife
concealed by a pillow.

Carefully, I get up every morning,
try not to disturb him.
He startles at the slightest sound,
doesn't recognize I'm his wife,
sees only enemy combatants
within every shadow.

Euthanasia

Each morning, I look
for my neighbor's dog, Oscar. Worry about the aging
hound, blind in one eye, growing thinner by the day,
so arthritic he's no longer able to stand
on his own, looks up in misery when I stop to pet him.

Miles away, my own mother dwindles.
Cancer consumes bones, organs, senses.
She curls like an anorexic fetus
in her hospital bed on an air mattress,
tumors filling her belly, mournfully
tells everyone who will listen
how she's finished, wants it to end.

I beg the higher power
to release life's stubborn hold,
deliver them both into easeful peace,
wish I could administer kind euthanasia.

Flashback

. . . the past is a country of darkness
—Danusha Lameris

I hide photo albums on a dusty shelf
in an unused room,
avoid past choices, former lives,
the skinny girl frozen
in a black and white snapshot.
Behind me, the tiny Seattle apartment
with asphalt tile floor,
minuscule galley kitchen,
claustrophobic bathroom
where I bled and miscarried.

Other pages display evidence
of isolated years in Neah Bay
among fishing shacks, dirt roads,
wandering herds of stray dogs
and feral horses.
Two shots capture
sun-bleached trailer house,
greasy spoon café
where I whirled milkshakes
and served tourists
burgers, berry pie a la mode,
earthenware bowls of clam chowder.

I remember playing canasta
with other military wives,
watching 16 mm movies
up in the rec deck.

Women shared washers and dryers
with young, single seamen.

Mostly, I flash back to choppers
landing on the concrete pad,
picking up zippered body bags
just outside my window.

Meditation

She sits there in what is left of the light.
—Francine Witte

During her final weeks before painful transition,
Mom sat by the living room window,
watched tiny birds as they picked at seeds
my cousin stuffed into a hanging nylon stocking.

This morning, hummingbirds cling to oak limbs
in our scarlet flowering front yard,
watch through rain-streaked glass
as I meditate, assemble fruit smoothies.

I wonder if wrens and bright-eyed sparrows
carry souls of prematurely lost loved ones,
spontaneously appear when needed to reassure
sagging spirits of despondent survivors.

Clearing Out

Every closet, cupboard, drawer reveals years of detritus:
Sunday offering envelopes, black and white family photos.
Invoices from an old kitchen remodel.
Copies of medical lab test results.
Bundles of decomposing rubber bands.
Spare hearing aid accessories.
Costume jewelry necklaces and earrings.
Six decades of changing fashions.
Shoes for every occasion.
Purses in multiple styles and colors.
Greeting cards and letters from deceased relatives.
Manuals and warranties for long-gone appliances.
Ticket stubs and bank deposit receipts.
Recent prescriptions, unused in their bottles.
A lined tablet with clinical details
of my dead mother's final tortuous day.

The Boxed-Up Dream

Inspired by a line from a Prartho Sereno poem

Disappointment poisoned mom's unrealized hopes.
World War II robbed her of dates, dances, romance.
Daily, her alcoholic, raging father reminded her
of the fairytale family she'd never possess.
I suspect she married my father to escape
the hell of poverty, domestic violence.
He fell short of the mate she imagined.
All he offered was love, laughter, and faithfulness,
nurturing devotion for his children and dogs,
coinage that, for her, held zero value.

During younger years,
I channeled her disillusionment.
Became an exhausted workaholic
who labored at two or three jobs,
every weekend, 60 or 70 hours per week.
Torpedoed career after career,
teacher, librarian, tech support rep.
Jogged into anorexia, osteoporosis.
Further destroyed two already-damaged husbands.

Now, in my seventh decade,
I take my foot off my own neck.
Accept aches and exhaustion.
Discover tranquility among irises,
roses, geraniums.
Appreciate quiet contentment
in rambling old home, blossoming garden.

Diatribes from the Afterlife

The dead are helpless. They can't make you
do things you don't want to do.
                              —Danusha Lameris

In dreams, my dead grandmother appears,
forces my mouth open, tries climbing inside.
During waking hours, I hear her voice
chiding me to turn off unused lights,
save stale bread heels,
roll my pasta dough thin.

Mom, eight years gone,
still scolds my failings,
laments divorces, transgressions.
She fusses over scandalous hair length,
bad choice of husbands,
refusal to plaster my face
with expensive makeup and lipstick.

My father refuses to comment.
I feel his happy-go-lucky aura
when I sit at his favorite Pacific Grove bench,
watch sunset from Lover's Point,
wet-suited surfers as they ride
curling waves, defy icy ocean.
From his side of the great divide,
he mutely shares my love for gardening,
dogs, trout streams in the Sierras.

Swimming Out of My Dreams

Inspired by a Lucille Lang Day poem

Deep sleep brings me back
to our family's orchard.
Weightless, I lift off from Central Valley soil,
windmill through spring sky
above almond tree blooms.

After landing, I breaststroke
across snow runoff canals,
then sun myself on broken concrete slabs,
sizzle and turn bronze
in one-hundred-degree heat.

Pet dogs from the past resurrect,
wag their tails as we wander
along ditch banks bursting with lupine,
revisit fuzz-filled summer air,
sagging peach limbs relieved
of harvested orbs.

Back at our fruit stand
built of wooden pallets
beside a rural highway
between Escalon and Modesto,
I peddle Dad's striped Texas melons,
cantaloupes, wrinkled yellow casabas.

All night I float through dioramas
of farm life in previous decades,
paddle toward sunrise
out of innocent dreams.

THE REAL STORY

*There's the story, then there's the real story,
then there's the story of how the story came to be told.
Then there's what you leave out of the story.
Which is part of the story too.*
—Margaret Atwood

Communion of Clumsy Sisters, Stumbling Souls

I am hungry and you give me a dictionary to decipher.
—Anne Sexton

I think of Eve
as she takes the first bite,
wipes suggestive juice
from soft, scarlet mouth.
Did she feel the hidden worm stir,
accept her guilty burden
with newly self-aware eyes?

Hungry Persephone opened
a blushing pomegranate
to ingest the fateful seed.
For penance, she forfeited sunlight,
condemned half a year
among the dead
in frigid underworld.

Each coveted feast,
honest articulation,
comes at a cost.
I share my truth,
let the chips fall,
kneel at appetite's altar.

Antidote

There is no such thing as gentle war. There is no peace that can't be flung aside. Our only enemy is that which make us enemies to each other.
—Amanda Gorman

Let us gather within sheltered lagoon,
contemplate women, children, elders
indiscriminately slaughtered by bombs.

Let us counteract malignant power lust,
trigger-happy hatred, propaganda-fueled rage,
call for peaceful solutions.

Instead of separation into opposing armies,
let us use voices and reason, set aside aggression,
act in the interests of common good.

Tonight, we launch tiny votives into tranquil Pacific,
illuminate encroaching darkness, offer hope,
serene but unyielding examples of grace.

Gaza 2023

Inspired by a Banksy social media meme

Riddled skeletons of ravaged buildings
circle smoking moonscape bomb crater.
Choking vapor infuses poisonous haze.

Empty swings cast somber shadows
of faceless children with outstretched arms,
scorched into ashy rubble.

Silhouettes of the incinerated
rend the heart, provoke the conscience,
innocent lives annihilated by war.

Hate Crime

*. . . mountains of men, oceans of bone,
an engine whose teeth shred all that is not our name*
—Tracy K. Smith

In Tennessee, white nationalists
brandish guns, threaten to murder
an eleven-year-old trans girl
whose traumatized parents contact the FBI,
hire a private investigator and security team.
When she boards the school bus,
friends shield her from jeers,
mob faces twisted with hate.

At an ultra-conservative conference
speakers call for eradication
of LBGT individuals.
In MAGA land, new regressive laws
play well with fascists in training,
have emboldened the crazies.

Red-hatted rabble
call themselves Christians,
cheer escalating cruelty,
embrace annihilation of anyone
unlike themselves.

Winter Solstice

Our country wobbles on a precipice.
Earth's poles tilt from distant sun.
Darkness, despair, overwhelm,
eclipse hopeful light.

It's the shortest day of the year.
Moody rain clouds obscure silver sky.
By 2 a.m., icy precipitation dislodges acorns,
streaks skylights, pelts bedroom windows.

Gale winds splinter blue eucalyptus,
topple fences, unshingle roofs.
In my blanket cocoon,
I wonder if dawn will ever unfold.

Illumination

Poetry can lamp an era scraped hollow
         —Amanda Gorman

Let us project light against darkness,
atone for carnage committed in our name,
cultivate a garden of nonviolence,
embrace kindness, inclusivity, respect.

Let us combine energy and optimism,
transform a war-ravaged world,
join hands and hearts,
nourish healing and hope.

Within this protected cove overlooking the Pacific,
we come together in common purpose,
launch a flotilla of commemorative luminaries,
envision a global community united in peace.

Imagine

Inspired by a social media meme attributed to Banksy

Two young boys stare at one another
through mirrored strands of barbed wire.
Exactly who is imprisoned is unclear,
a matter of subjective perspective.
Israeli/Palestinian children bleed
the same shade of crimson.
Bombs, bullets, grenades rip flesh,
eradicate life without regard
to nationalistic designation.

Imagine an invasion of empathy,
pandemic spread of compassion,
collaboration replacing annihilation.
Run terrorism's horror movie in reverse,
innocent babies, the elderly and infirm revived,
hatred extinguished,
supportive community restored.

Peace Lanterns

The use of the atomic bomb, with its indiscriminate killing of women and children, revolts my soul.
—Herbert Hoover

Let us gather, light candles,
observe a moment of silence,
remember the victims,
repudiate atrocities
executed under our name.

Let us stand on Pacific shore,
envision hands joined in creation
rather than unconscionable acts
of hatred, tearing apart.

Let us illuminate hearts
in quiet affirmation of non-violence,
ignite peace lanterns, fold paper cranes,
treat our neighbors
as we wish to be considered,
vow to make war obsolete.

Shadow Government

Purchased by an unelected oligarch
as part of a hostile takeover,
democracy teeters, then starts to fall,
hollowed out by mass firings,
dismantling agencies and departments,
infiltration of government databases
by teenage incels.

Old white men mistake *The Handmaid's Tale*
as an instructional manual,
introduce legislation to prevent women
from exercising the right to vote
or control their own bodies.

Daily, I doom-scroll headlines,
ponder each unfolding outrage,
wonder how to prevent ongoing assaults
against established rule of law,
separation of powers.

I resist and speak out,
refuse to concede
or bend the knee
to corrupt egomaniacs
who are stealing my country.

Smudge

After mom died,
my cousin burned sage,
smudged every room
in the house
to erase lingering pain
from traumatic transition.

Across the street,
a neighbor ignites silvery leaves
crumbled into an abalone shell,
wafts smoke indoors,
around yard perimeter,
effaces her intolerant brother's
cruel political ravings.

How I wish we could kindle
healing bonfires around the world,
eliminate evil energy,
offer our sick planet a cure
for hatred, oppression,
purify our souls,
deliver spiritual ablation.

Storm Front

The latest atmospheric river
swirls wind, thunder, lightning
across blue, contused sky.
Sparrows shelter in manzanita.
Clouds of tattered blackbirds
circle rooftops, disappear
within dripping pines.

In the kitchen, I mobilize brain cells
with mugs of black coffee,
doom scroll through headlines
that describe the demise
of civility, morality, democracy.

In younger, healthier years
I would have been out in the streets
with outraged activist friends.
Unified, we would chant,
carry picket signs,
occupy government offices,
do our best to shut down the machine.

My older, less resilient self
relies on phone calls, petitions,
refuses to roll over and accept
the avalanche of deportations,
defunding, firings, web sites
scrubbed of statistics and fact.

As our country retreats to the time
of corrupt robber barons,

I join white-haired contemporaries
who have nothing left to lose.
We write letters, meet with legislators,
hold their feet to the fire.

The Real Story

This is a fairytale where the ending
is neither happy nor everlasting,
only trapped in a coma.

Rapunzel develops alopecia.
Cinderella's glass slipper cracks.
Bipolar Prince Charming reverts to an ogre.

Beauty and her Beast
unite to bequeath future progeny
flawed DNA.

Briars spring from poisoned earth.
The castle moat widens,
magic mirror darkens.

A Cold Coyote Always Returns

Every month or so,
when his old lady evicts him
or my name comes up next
on his rolodex list,
he comes,
needing twenty bucks till payday,
my understanding,
to be scratched,
fucked and fed.
I learn to think of him
like the neighborhood tomcat,
rubbing up against my ankles,
wanting a fresh bowl of milk
and a warm place to crash.
I touch him,
love him,
persuade myself I have
an exotic new house pet.
After twenty minutes,
the purring quits and
he's all nerves and claws,
ready to resume his prowling,
wanting outside.
By daybreak,
he's talking how
we've gotta keep things
symbiotic.
Have no expectations,
he repeatedly says.

One kiss later,
that damned Coyote
takes four cookies
and my car keys,
disappears out the door.

Where Trickster Lurks

Inside the classroom,
Coyote tosses spitballs,
makes farting noises,
draws a bloodshot eye
on the back of his hand.

Later, at Mozzi's Saloon,
he smashes dead soldiers,
crushes beer cans
against his forehead,
grabs a bar maid,
trips the bus boy,
throws peanut shells
onto the floor.

He hacks passwords,
crashes hard drives,
takes down the NSA
with pornographic spam.

Pisses inside
a prominent senator's shoes.
Takes a crap
on the House speaker's
best suit.

Posts sex tapes
with televangelists
and child prostitutes
all over YouTube.

Tarnished Grail

Guinevere wonders
if all marriages
start in passion,
grow anemic over time,
end up going stale.

She and Arthur find
less and less to discuss,
sleep apart, go their
separate ways, have
no common dreams.

When she needs him,
he is carousing with the boys,
crusading for another lost cause,
leaves her rattling around,
untouched, in his
drafty stone house.

The day Lancelot
slithers onto the scene,
all French flash with
his courtly attentions,
is it any surprise
he catches her eye,
sweet forbidden fruit,
the seductive snake,
an untended garden?

Fractured Fairytale

Pan to garden bower for lovers
gilded with jasmine.
Cut to palace ballroom.
Cue the scene of a fairytale ending.

Unfortunately, happy-ever-after
is the element missing.
This stage is set for
a slow-motion train wreck.
Prince Charming snores,
reverted to frog form.
Comatose, he slides
from throne to floor
after bong hits, martinis.

Cinderella enables,
hides his empties,
manufactures excuses.
She cleans up after accidents,
maintains appearances,
afraid to tip off the servants.

Their performance grinds on.
An admission of truth
would fracture the kingdom.

Windmills

White pinwheels line
the Salinas Valley, Altamount Pass.
Giant propellers spin in gusty wind,
transform breeze into electrical power.

Passing them, I think of Don Quixote,
deluded knight errant
confronting monsters
created by foggy eyes, failing mind,
a pathetic joke to observers.

As climate change, wars,
toxic political cultists
poison earth and existence,
I sign petitions, write letters,
fear my efforts will be equally futile.

WHEN WE DON'T SEE IT

*We don't see things as they are,
we see them as we are.*
—Anais Nin

When We Don't See It

Sickle moon cloaks itself
in silvery folds of crystalline fog.
Its ghostly corona spills pearly glow
across spiraling galaxy
littered with streaking comets.

Night sky hides orbiting constellations
behind atmospheric river storm clouds,
chunks of hail, wind-propelled sleet.
Lunar shape-shifter swells,
disappears within ebony cosmos,
flickering chips of stellar debris.

Shivering and Shedding

Inspired by a Mary Kay Rummel poem

Along neighborhood streets, elms and sycamores shiver,
rattle red foliage as the first autumn rainstorm
blusters inland from ocean.
Scarlet dianthus fade, spill shuttlecock seed heads.
Volunteer marigolds droop wizened faces.

In family orchards, late season peaches
shed soft, blushing projectiles.
Shaken almond limbs dump golden, rattling bounty.
Exhausted vineyards droop, weep Tokay clusters.

Geese lift from wetlands, flap across September sky,
complain in unison now that summer is over.
I bag up castoffs, dead-head hydrangeas,
clean oak leaf-clogged gutters.

Washing Death Out of Your Ears

Another old classmate bites the dust. Succumbs to heart attack,
cancer, bullet through the brain,
just sick of living.

Parents are gone, uncles dead, cousins in chemotherapy,
Befuddled aunts suffering
from progressive dementia.

Each day, another body part dislocates, breaks or malfunctions.
Funerals, memorials, wakes
replace wild kegger parties.

Sad obituaries supplant optimistic predictions,
laundry lists of achievements
from antique high school annuals.

A friend announces her final meal will be
raw kernels of popcorn, something
to startle mourners at her crematorium service.

I'm holding out
for an erotic poetry rave: blues, bad boys and blinis
as my exiting swan song.

Consider Yourself Lucky

As you settle into a rental cabin
surrounded by sociable deer,
twitchy squirrels, twisted oak forest,
you contemplate the good fortune
of inheriting money
to finance temporary escape.

You bake fragrant quiche Lorraine,
sip chilled Pellegrino,
spill poetry onto blank pages
at a pull-out wooden table.
Two spoiled dogs snuggle in their little beds
near fireplace and sofa.

Last time you were here—
dying father, failing mom,
raging alcoholic husband,
unraveling love,
crumbling marriage.

This year, you are a fortunate woman,
anticipate a week of hiking,
photography, meditation.
A peaceful interlude within which to heal,
finally read that stack of books you've been saving.

Road Trip

I vow not to burden myself
with unneeded possessions,
pack a change of clothes,
books, laptop computer.
I drive beyond Soledad, Paso Robles,
pass a lush patchwork of vineyards.
Unwanted responsibilities
vanish behind me

Wineries and tasting rooms
burgeon along west-bound highway.
At the summit, I look south,
admire Moro Rock
wreathed in foggy shawl
as it protrudes from
turquoise ocean.

Moonstone Beach Bar & Grill
provides an exotic brunch replete
with champagne I cannot drink
after losing both urge and habit.
Today my greatest desire
is to contemplate ephemeral clouds,
silent rain of falling pine needles.

I explore the sensation
of being emotionally untethered,
allow the ache of intentional loneliness
to penetrate and surround,
tell myself to expand and explore,
seek prophetic omens
within oaken forest.

Fluidity

The human spirit is made from water
—Jorge Luis Borges

I surface from sleep,
splash dry face, rinse scratchy eyes,
shuffle to the kitchen,
swallow my daily ration of pills.

Outside, mist drips from incoming fog.
Spider webs sparkle with liquid diamonds.
Puddles collect beneath olive tree,
saturate sodden ground.

Rivulets from the neighbor's broken sprinkler
glitter as precious water is wasted.
Renegade outflow gurgles downhill,
transports rafts of rose petals, twigs.

From time to time,
sunlight burns through low-lying clouds.
Ocean breeze ruffles sage and manzanita.
Temperature rises, falls, rockets skyward again.

It's a typical summer morning,
Coastal weather shaped by central valley heat
as nature's air conditioning
pulls moist miasma over beaches and dunes.

Heat Dome

Summer's morning fog deceives.
Damp mantle billows inland,
embellishes Monterey pines
in dripping diamonds.

Minimal shore breeze flutters
lank berried limbs
of blood-red manzanita.
Feeble wind offers zero respite.

By noon, denim sky bakes.
Fire-eyed sun sizzles,
irradiates cobblestone driveway,
transforms sidewalks to griddles.

The dogs and I wilt, shelter in shadows,
recline in front of oscillating fans,
press bare skin against cool tile floor,
chug-a-lug icy gallons of water.

Rockaway Ramble

In Pacifica, beach cottages hunker
above fissured, crumbling cliffs,
nestle among yellow mustard,
pink and white radish explosions.

Spindrift-tipped cobalt waves
batter guano-stained boulders.
Wet-suited surfers paddle waxed boards
beyond jagged monoliths into rough water.

My mate and I
ramble flowering trail
between golden hillsides.

A cotton-tail bunny cautiously peers
from hemlock and yarrow.
Above us, a shifting kaleidoscope
of slanting sunrays, then gray, drippy fog.

The headland trail we explore is lined
with memorial gardens, blooming geraniums,
nasturtium, purple artichokes.

We time-travel backwards,
revisit grammar school,
old family home,
site of first teenage kiss.

We celebrate survivorship,
mourn our losses,
marvel at how love persists.

Shivers

Love, like a mountain-wind upon an oak,
Falling upon me, shakes me leaf and bough.
　　　　　　—Sappho, "Love"

In our office, my husband's strong hands
knead knotted shoulders as I wrestle poetry from laptop.
Erotically distracted, his touch makes me tremble.

Beneath the desk, a tan and cream rescue dog
gazes up with loving eyes, squeaks a soggy toy.
When declared a good boy, his fluffy tail quivers.

Backyard roses flourish in sunshine.
Nourished by compost, recent rain, daily affirmations,
twisted wisteria dangles lavender flowers.

Afternoon breezes shudder inland from ocean,
erase fog banks, ruffle Monterey pines,
spill squawking blue jays from shivering branches.

The Graduate

I was seventeen
the summer Anne Bancroft
seduced Dustin Hoffman
on the big screen.
My fiancée took me to see it,
then drove us to a seedy motel
where he rented a room.

A male friend who was also a teen
when the film came out
said it changed his life.
Suddenly, his mom's middle-aged friends
started hitting on him.

Watching the final escape scene
with Benjamin and Elaine grinning
from the back of the bus,
I want to warn them running away
buys only temporary freedom.

The daily grind
tempers passionate love.
Happy endings never last.
We all end up scarred.

Entering the Temple of Words

Carefully follow creativity's roadmap
transmitted through dreams.
Pause at a shrine of shelves
holding poetry by Adrienne Rich,
Annie Dillard, Mary Oliver.

Silently recite finely crafted verses.
Marvel how they commingle
image, imagination, and metaphor,
weave a tapestry more enormous
than the sum of its parts.

Be very still.
Slow your breathing.
Look within.
Listen to what your soul
wishes to tell you.
Find a quiet corner.
Let the poem stretch,
achieve its potential.

Genuflect to the muse.

Her Barefooted Gypsy Soul

Inspired by a Prartho Sereno poem

Geriatric, former wild-child goddesses,
we gift ourselves with monthly poetry lunches,
filterless political commentary,
dress in technicolor caftans, tie-dye tunics,
dangling crystal pendants.

Bohemians to the core,
we frequent Big Sur hangouts:
Nepenthe, Deetjen's,
Henry Miller Memorial Library,
preferably under redwoods
or on shady deck.

Over the years, hips and knees fail.
Eyesight worsens. Wrinkles accumulate.
Memory and cognitive abilities falter.
Passion for blinis, ambrosia burgers,
as well as admiration of Anais Nin,
Adrienne Rich, and their daring
writer sisters remains.

The Only Train in Town

Western Pacific train tracks
crisscross the perimeters
of Central Valley jerkwater towns.
At night, shrieking whistles
herald passage of huffing locomotives
as they haul tractors, cattle, ag chemicals
from Sacramento to Fresno,
Bakersfield and beyond.

Children would ignore parental warnings,
jump between wooden ties,
scavenge corroded iron spikes,
place pennies to be flattened
by churning metal wheels
chugging down steel rails.

Railroad spurs to freight docks
at the Escalon Packers cannery
allowed pallets of fruit cocktail,
fancy sliced peaches, tomato purée
to be loaded, then transported
to grocery warehouses
throughout the U.S.

Sometimes auto drivers would challenge
descending wooden arms
at clanging crossings
to avoid being trapped for hours
by long lines of uncoupled cars.

We'd read obituaries in the local paper
for those who miscalculated and lost.

Decades later, I still hear
screaming diesel engines in recurrent dreams,
creaking undercarriage complaints,
braying whistle stop groans.

February Transition

Where did winter go
while we were distracted
by cupboards and closets?
For days, we are hammered
by gale winds, toppled trees,
torrential rain, power loss,
massive flooding.

After a wild night of gusts
cruelly wrenching our awnings,
yellow daffodils unfurl.
Morning sun reveals scrubbed horizon.
Radiant light awakens oxalis, azaleas,
pronged foliage of purple crocus,
fragrant pink hyacinths.

I creak from bed sheets,
throw back blackout curtains,
inventory puddled patio, ice-blue bearded iris,
cowled calla lilies, shattered oak limbs,
rejoice at emerging marigolds and lobelia,
sweep away passing atmospheric river's
sodden left-behind wreckage.

Remembering How to Fly

Invisible wings unfurl within dream,
lift me above popcorn blooms
of spring almond fields,
allow me to effortlessly soar
across Ventana Wilderness.

Despite being terrified of heights,
I have never felt more at peace,
admire aerial views of redwoods,
weightlessly swoop over stucco bungalows,
steepled barns, Spanish tile roofs.

I wake to morning stiffness,
arthritic aches and pains.
Bills, housework, the need
to pull garden weeds
drag me back down to earth.

Energy flags, aging joints and eyes fail.
I look forward to launching soul beyond flesh,
a human caterpillar jettisoning its husk,
spreading feathered pinions to become one
with limitless celestial realms.

Conundrum

Why do lyrics
of a sour cream commercial
loop endlessly, day and night,
inside my septuagenarian brain?

I can't recall items on my grocery list,
barely pass a cognition test at the doctor's,
yet am unable to disremember
"Everything tastes better with a dollop of Daisy,"
no matter how hard I try.

After napping to a Hallmark Christmas movie
during cold afternoon,
jolly jingle merges seamlessly
with first verse of
Hark, the Herald Angels Sing.

Age brings multiplying challenges:
dislocating a finger while changing fitted sheets,
constant arthritic ache,
numb arm, frozen shoulder,
the sensation of walking into a brick wall
each day by 1:30 p.m.

In a recliner on two heating pads,
I close my eyes, meditate, seek serenity,
hear the refrain "Hold the pickles, hold the lettuce,
special orders don't upset us,"
place an urgent prayer
for a painless ad-free hour of peace.

Summons

We snake our way around yellow hibiscus,
stroll through lava rock grotto,
admire ferns, white orchids,
climb to volcanic ridge,
watch the day bloom.

A bronze rooster with scarlet tail feathers
perches on mossy edge of abalone shell fishpond,
crows until morning sun hauls its burning mass
above pink horizon into cloudless blue sky.

Khaki hens emerge from split-leaf philodendron,
gather drowsy offspring for ground-scratching tutorial.
Self-important cockerels square off, raise their hackles,
strut plush expanse of beach-resort lawn.

An incoming cruise ship navigates Lihue harbor,
plows frothy wake across turquoise lagoon.
Serenity stills my soul, offers dove seraphs.
Paddle boarders stroke toward palm-framed shore.
Sunrise surfer threads spindrift curl of incoming wave.

Sunset Dinner at Happy Talk Bar & Grill

We mutiny after seeing cauliflower steak
listed for $40 on the menu
of a trendy Kaua'i restaurant
where we'd made reservations
for our anniversary dinner.

Instead, we backtrack to Hanalei Bay Resort,
score a corner table at Happy Talk Bar & Grill,
mingle with mourning doves and Nene geese,
admire a million-dollar view through vistas
of palm trees, orchids, rose bougainvillea.

Virgin pina coladas set the mood.
We order sashimi appetizers,
a smash burger, fish tacos.
Locals on keyboard and drums
crowd the tiny stage,
perform covers of favorite songs
from the 70s and 80s.

As sunset paints Napali hills gold,
overhead rainclouds turn pink and yellow.
You hold my hand, kiss my palm.
We sing along with familiar lyrics,
splurge on a gargantuan wedge
of strawberry cheesecake.

Ichabod Egret

Halloween morning, Princeville, Kaua'i

Disgruntled white curmudgeon
hunches disheveled, feathery wings,
dispiritedly trudges
through fallen orange blossoms.

When a pair of Nene geese intrude,
he swivels his head,
throws some serious side-eye,
hisses a warning.

Red-crested cardinals
peck at giant African snails,
forage wherever they please,
simply ignore him.

Skinny shanked, straw-legged
Ichabod Crane imposter
grumps his cranky way
across sodden Sleepy Hollow golf course.

Incel

Bachelor Nene goose stakes out territory
among ferns beside the swimming pool
where he screeches and patrols,
pursues feathered invaders.

At 3 am I hear him caterwauling
from the lawn below our balcony,
shrieks his grievances to the stars,
wakes up sleeping tourists.

By morning, he has melted
into a feathery mound of misery
beneath a clump of red ginger
where doves, hens and roosters avoid him.

When I pass his personal pity party,
he uncoils a serpentine neck.
Ebony beak strikes.
He malevolently hisses.

Rainy Day Rooster

Bedraggled rooster struts
around resort swimming pool.
Puddled rainwater sluices him
as it pours from sodden umbrella.

Hens and chicks show better judgement,
ride out passing storm,
shelter beneath elephant-ear philodendron
within jungle thickets.

Thunderheads darken misty horizon.
Paddle boarders return to shore.
Lightning splinters charcoal sky,
pierces writhing bay.

My mate insists on swimming laps
despite tropical downpour.
I take cover under sturdy roof
of a wooden gazebo.

What Is Unseen

What we see and what we don't.
    —Jane Hirshfield

Ceiling fan fails to dispel humid darkness.
Outside, Nene Geese
hunker under dripping ti plants.
Roosters assemble below coconut palm trees,
eager to crow, raise the sun.

Despite sporadic downpour,
I wander the winding pathway
among plumeria, rainbow eucalyptus.
Tiny chicks twitter,
hidden by hibiscus and scarlet ginger.

A storm front persists,
foments whitecaps and thunderheads.
Grey mist and zero visibility
camouflage tropical depression's
soggy advance into Hanalei Bay.

I stand on a bluff overlooking Bali Hai,
lament no-show sunrise.
Warm deluge sluices ashore.
Mourning doves vanish.
Tempestuous winds dismember
my flimsy umbrella.

SACRED SPACE

*Your sacred space is where you can find yourself
again and again.*
—Joseph Campbell

Autumn Avalanche

Chunky blue jay clutches groaning elm limb.
Feathered agitator triggers scarlet leaf deluge.
September breeze carries summer's cast-offs
into drifts to become spicy compost.

Golden sycamore leaves cartwheel underfoot
as I wander neighborhood sidewalks.
Woodpeckers deposit acorns
within beak-bored holes riddling power poles.

In the garden, squirrels stash nuts and seeds.
I restock bookshelves, pantry,
pack away cool, cotton sheets,
shed August tank top, drag out sweatshirts.

Super Moon

Luminosity lasers through shaggy redwoods,
outshines a spattering of glittery stars,
ascends to hang against celestial ceiling.

Fluffy ageratum floats below ebony sky.
Super moon transforms shadowy rose garden
into fragrant pink and yellow pinpoints.

Unable to submerge into stupor,
I abandon bedroom, join nocturnal foragers,
bathe bare skin within lunar light.

Pre-Dawn Meditation

It came to us, like the crazed spirit of a light-stunned god
                              —Mary Kay Rummel

A higher power whispers affirmations in my ear
as I slice pineapple, berries, melon
into a plastic tumbler,
blend fruity chunks with almond milk,
create nourishing smoothies.

On the counter, the coffee pot awakens,
drips scalding water over ground mocca java.
Hot joe perfumes the kitchen.
Hungry dogs circle my feet.
Awakening sky blossoms.
Burning sun rises.

Already I hear dueling hummingbirds
among front yard sage,
whirring avian clash among crimson blossoms.
I list today's obligations, read a friend's poetry
while nibbling a muffin, scribble possibilities,
parrot Mary Oliver's bolstering mantras.

Sodden Spring

Charcoal parfait streaks silver horizon,
overlays ascending gold sun.
Lavender lupine explodes
from last week's desiccated branches.
Wind wallops Monterey Bay
into navy breakers shedding spindrift,
flings careening sea gulls
from roiling skies.

In drowned garden
trumpet-faced jonquils
gyrate, break their own necks.
Thirty-mile-an-hour gusts
buffet centenarian oak,
contort groaning cypress.
Vanquished freesia scatter white petals
onto soil transformed to soupy peat
by back-to-back storms.

Gutters swell, overflow.
Storm wreckage spins downhill
toward flooded intersection
where afternoon commuters
hydroplane along saturated asphalt,
pause, uncertain how to proceed
through a sodden, congested crossing
once controlled by now-powerless lights.

Morning's Surprise

Gold bleeds around kitchen curtains.
Peach sunlight leaks between angular pines.
I rinse overripe blackberries,
blend them with spinach, pineapple, melon,
healthy buffer to handfuls of pills.

When I open front door to let out the dogs,
hummingbirds chirrup, explode from silver sage,
dive-bomb whoever interrupts fuchsia feasting.
Red squirrels tight wire across power lines,
descend telephone pole, invade patio, yard.

On the corner, adolescent wild turkeys gather,
scuff aside mulch to breakfast on grubs.
Cotton-tail bunnies disappear inside sticky monkey snarls.
I meander sandy trail toward glistening beach,
admire lupine bounty, meditate upon whispering surf.

Embezzlement

Blustery waves,
churned by storm winds,
unravel surf, fling mounds
of transient foam.

Thieving tides incrementally
pilfer gold sand,
leave behind broken pebbles,
deeply carved stone.

Ravaged beach erodes to bedrock
as raving ocean sluices inland,
invades and embezzles
what's left of high ground.

Wetland Concert

Down in the shaded woods by Crow Creek,
Brown-eyed Susan is awake now and singing
—Diane Porter

Sunflowers border meandering trail.
Their scratchy leaves blow in ocean breeze,
a whispery summer percussion.
Yellow mustard erupts along muddy sedge.
Laden willow limbs groan under sparrows.

Lizards skitter beneath silver sage,
golden sonatas of fluttering poppies.
Tule berms part as a green-headed mallard,
his mate, and phalanx of ducklings emerge,
perform a squawking refrain.

An irate gander hisses at joggers.
Red-wing blackbirds and gulls
chirp, chatter, quarrel.
Bullfrogs conclude wetland concert
with a bass beatbox coda.

Garden of Weedin'

*I stare at the unweeded garden
and think of all I have stopped doing.*
—Emilie Lygren

After rain, spurge and oxalis sprout,
squeeze out alyssum, efface steppingstones,
burrow under backyard fence,
fringe both sides of my driveway.

Morning sunshine germinates guilt.
I pluck weeds from garden mulch,
deadhead yellow roses, pink geraniums,
snap the necks of spent bearded iris.

With pruning shears I decapitate
fading Pride of Madeira spires,
fill our green bin with oak duff, dry leaves,
tangled mats of chrysanthemum wreckage.

A neighbor ignores grass tufts, dandelions, thistles,
sips afternoon wine with friends at her patio table,
hangs a rustic sign on one ragged bush:
Welcome to my Garden of Weedin!

Scarlet Reminders

Sometimes it is necessary
to reteach a thing its loveliness.
　　　　　—Galway Kinnell

Teal-throated hummingbirds dip scarlet heads,
sip from crimson salvia goblets,
probe cerise cactus blooms,
siphon sugary nectar.

Copper sunrise haloes tender leaves
of red-trunked manzanita.
Berry clusters dangle from russet limbs,
offer temptation to foraging sparrows.

In morning kitchen,
I slice watermelon, strawberries,
the tip of one clumsy finger,
watch searing solar star
hoist itself above shifting fog banks.

Ocean wind litters brick walkway
with ruby casualties of brutal gusts,
garnet petals ripped from miniature roses,
torn geranium splatters.

Liberation

I rest in the grace of the world and am free
                                —Wendell Berry

Egg yolk oxalis overruns every garden.
Yellow blooms crowd blue ceanothus,
lavender lupine, damp miner's lettuce.
Orange poppies ignore boundaries,
invade divider strips, front yards,
cracked cement driveways.

I soak in sunlight's vitamin D,
slowly stroll neighborhood streets,
inhale ocean breeze,
admire pink flowering crab apples,
white calla lilies.
Meditative doves nest
among star jasmine tangles.

Passing beneath shadowy canopy
of moss bearded oak limbs
loaded with blackbirds,
I cherish freedom to wander,
am rewarded by a volunteer clump
of tiny gold jonquils.

Sacred Space

Volunteer calla lilies
interrupt bursting cat tails,
stretch beyond budding willows
gather spring equinox sunshine.

Laguna Grande pond
showcases a braying aquacade
of floating Canada geese,
a minnow-spearing blue heron.

Mud ducks and their fluffy progeny
parade along rutted trail
as I commune with wetland spirits,
savor serenity among feathery brethren.

Hummingbirds at Sunrise

Nectar sippers appear at dawn,
bypass salvia to perch on oak twigs,
peer through kitchen window
as I blend morning smoothies.

Midday, red-crowned hummingbirds
hover above late fall's climbing roses,
then vanish behind manzanita berries and leaves,
migrate to a neighbor's flowering garden.

At twilight, jeweled sprites probe purple sage,
halo my head while I sprinkle peruvian lilies.
Darting colibri descend to reveal
secret trove of night-blooming jasmine.

Crows

Precursors of elusive rainfall,
glossy black harbingers
shriek from power lines and tree limbs,
delve into oak leaf-clogged gutters.

They strut across front yard,
tip over bird bath.
When challenged by dogs,
grumpy avians pigeon-toe
toward white picket fence,
flap just beyond jaw reach.

As dark storm clouds
contuse against sweaty horizon,
another airborne murder descends,
replaces the ebony battalion
currently frisking soggy garden for insects.

From my kitchen,
I watch crows descend,
invade unsuspecting neighborhood,
congregate on rooftops to sharpen beaks,
plot nefarious plunders.

Fiscalini Ranch Birding

Cobweb thistles groan
beneath feathery weight of twittering
sparrows, phoebes and finches.

Turkey vultures spread black wings,
circle above frantic voles,
send them diving down hidden burrows.

Great Blue heron
launches himself aloft,
glides across misty meadow.

Big bird flops to an ungainly landing
along crumbling bluff edge
among dead lupine wreckage.

Golden-eyed goliath patrols adobe trail.
Snakelike neck uncoils as he strikes.
Stiletto beak spears morning breakfast.

Sun Dog

Sunrise spotlights vaporous arch,
brackets granite boulders,
spindrift cameo,
reshapes mist into albino rainbow.

As haloed star ascends,
raccoon marauders conclude hidden mischief,
vanish silently into ragged clumps
of seer, dwindling lupine.

Deer herds ignore the celestial spectacle,
parade between houses,
forage in garbage cans, front yards,
migrate uphill into aging pine forest.

First Light

Gold spills through charcoal clouds,
outlines scarlet branched manzanita,
frilly white bearded iris.
As sunlight warms steaming garden,
bejeweled hummingbirds guzzle
from purple Pride of Madeira.

Rain retreats behind blue mountains
for a few brilliant hours.
Along weighted tree leaves,
puddled drops glitter.
Emerald grass sprouts
from moist mulch.
The first daffodils unfurl.

In quiet kitchen, I sip hot mocha java,
meditate as dogs munch crunchy kibble,
watch technicolor horizon
through streaky windows.
Morning pushes aside thunderheads,
pulses orange, pink, and amber.

Tunnel of Moonlight

Moonlight tunnels through ebony cosmos,
tumbles toward silent wetlands,
inscribes a wavy platinum ribbon
across obsidian pond.

Lunar glow silhouettes pliant willows,
scotch broom thickets,
illuminates Rastafarian blackberry tangles,
reveals duck and goose nests.

All night, sickle planetoid
circumscribes star-pocked celestial ceiling,
spills silver over bent trees, looping trail,
instigates frog song from espresso lagoon.

Recovery

After a night of howling wind,
atmospheric river projectiles,
icy rain strafes skylights.
French doors bulge in morning tempest.
I wake to cold house,
cypress debris cluttering streets,
fallen fences, severed power lines
absence of electrical service.

The giant blue eucalyptus
half a block away
sags, groans, and splinters.
Shattered limbs, pungent foliage
bury my neighbor's driveway,
barely miss his new, silver Tesla.

For two days, we shiver,
drag out extra blankets,
rely on battery powered candles,
lament thawing groceries.
I heat water on gas stove top,
brew coffee, create a skimpy breakfast
of caffeine and instant oatmeal.

Later, with unwashed hair,
unshaven legs,
I navigate ravaged Carmel Beach,
accept my sister's kind invitation,
enjoy a long, steamy shower
in her rented hotel room.

Willing Suspension of Disbelief

Window on the Bay glitters with frost.
Blue and green tents of the homeless
lean against ceanothus, coast chaparral.
In the marina, porcupine masts
pierce blue denim sky.
Above Del Monte Beach
dangles a leafless eucalyptus limb
entangled within invisible spider web.
It hangs above sand and sage,
below feathery clouds.

It's thirty-eight degrees, early January;
arthritic hips throb.
I persevere, give thanks for padded vest,
zippered jacket, thick woolen gloves.
Trail-walking companions stroll between
rising sun, thrashing ocean.
We trust warm days will return,
golden poppies, purple lupine
will eventually sprout.

About the Author

Jennifer Lagier, M.A., M.L.I.S., Ph.D., lives a block from the stage where Bob Dylan and Joan Baez performed at the Monterey Folk Festival in 1963, and Jimi Hendrix torched his guitar in 1967. She served as Area Coordinator and an instructor with California Poets in the Schools, taught at Modesto Junior College, California State University, Monterey Bay, Hartnell College, and Monterey Peninsula College.

Jennifer has published twenty-five books and has work appearing in a variety of anthologies and literary magazines. A former editor for the *Homestead Review,* she now edits the *Monterey Poetry Review* and helps publicize Monterey Bay Poetry Consortium readings.

Website: jlagier.net
Facebook: www.facebook.com/JenniferLagier/

www.ingramcontent.com/pod-product-compliance
Lightning Source LLC
Chambersburg PA
CBHW022015160426
43197CB00007B/435